Dedicated to Ngonidzashe Paul Duncan Maturure

Alexia Press

FOR YOU...WITH LOVE

AUSTIN MACAULEY PUBLISHERS™

LONDON · CAMBRIDGE · NEW YORK · SHARJAH

A CIP catalogue record for this title is available from the British Library.

ISBN 9781788482486 (Paperback)
ISBN 9781788482493 (Hardback)
ISBN 9781788482509 (E-Book)

www.austinmacauley.com

First Published (2018)
Austin Macauley Publishers Ltd
25 Canada Square
Canary Wharf
London
E14 5LQ

Introduction

To everything, there is a season; a time to be born and a time to die; a time to plant and a time to pluck out what is planted. Ecclesiastes 3: 1-2.

What really inspired me to write this book to you, my son, is this:

I don't know what goes through your mind when you think about the loss of your father which happened before you were even old enough to remember him. I hope that you are constantly reminded that I am here to answer any questions you might have about him.

I must add that as the years go by, you grow up to look a lot like him.

You have achieved a great deal in your young life and I have confidence that you will have the success that you always talk about. You are intelligent, mature, respectful and ambitious.

I want this book to be a reminder to you of courage, hope, faith, patience, endurance, forgiveness and above all, love.

I need you to read it to find out more about your past, but most importantly, to make you understand how present God is in your life and how to seek him first in all you do in your life, for He is the way, the truth and the life.

It is true that an event in one's life can either make or break him. Most of these events are those that take place during the early years of childhood, where comprehension is harder to master.

I guess what I am trying to say is that I cannot change the course of your life, but I should be able to pick up the pieces and help you make sense of all that has happened in your life, leading to today.

I want you to know that it is my duty as a surviving parent to ensure that the loss of your dad at an early age does not bring you a feeling that you are unworthy of having a male role model in your life.

I can imagine the emptiness you feel inside of you sometimes. I know that you cry sometimes when you think about what could have been if he were still alive, or if you had shared more years with him.

I know that as we grow older, we yearn to know more about our parents, both living and deceased, as we often want to avoid making the mistakes they made or alternatively are overcome by a need to walk in their footsteps, if they have been influential in any way.

God has been faithful to me that is why I feel that such matters are not ones to take lightly. I asked Him for guidance before I started writing this book and throughout the entire process.

One of my fears is that I don't want you to only be successful on the outside for the world to see; I know you will be successful. I want you to also be successful on the inside.

You can achieve this by always remembering that your father needed not be alive today for you to feel his love. He never left you and I say this with the greatest confidence as I know the love he had for you. Never forget that.

Here is what I know for sure. If he were alive today, you would have someone to share your trading ambitions with, which I know nothing about. You would have someone to go cycling with, someone to watch all the Black American movies with, listen to the music that goes with all that and certainly, a gym buddy, as he also took a great liking for his physical fitness.

I know you miss him even if you don't remember him. Taking all this into consideration, you have excelled in school, have become a role model to your younger brothers. You are a true leader amongst your friends and demonstrated a sense of maturity beyond your age.

I want you to pick up this book on those days when you feel happy on the outside and so sad on the inside. God knows we all experience those. I want you to know that it is okay to feel empty because you miss your father, but never ever feel empty because you think you were not worthy of a father.

It is okay to feel depressed at some of life's outcomes. But don't be depressed about your past. A past is important to remember because we all need to remember where God has taken us from and placed us.

Wherever you go, remember that you are God's creation and made in his own image.

You may not understand why God took him away from you when you were so young. You may even feel anger and a sense of being robbed of the love of a father. I understand all that. I understand too, that I went through the same feelings when I remembered how absent my mother was in my life. But today, I am able to relate with you in this feeling.

I know that it is my God-given responsibility to spend each day of my life, moulding you and your brothers into the God-fearing future husbands and fathers of your future households, by way of showing you how to love, forgive, care and respect.

It is my God-given responsibility to demonstrate to you how to embrace heartaches and teach you how to overcome them so that you do not hold any resentment.

It is my God-given responsibility to tell you the truth always, for God is the truth.

It is my God-given responsibility to pray for you each day for God's love to prevail in your lives. Prayer has been the greatest weapon for me and if I do not say that to you with the greatest affirmation, then I have taught you nothing.

It is my God-given responsibility to listen to you even when you feel like no one else is listening; and on the same token, be the distinct voice you hear when the voices of the world are echoing simultaneously in your ears.

It is my God-given responsibility to teach you to forgive and to show you that it is okay to get angry and say words we don't mean, as it is in those outbursts that we really get to know what's inside the heart. By extending an invitation to sit down and talk through after you have said hurtful words to me, I hope you remember that it was in those words that I grew to know exactly what was inside you and behind that smile.

That encouraged me to ignore the pain the words caused and instead, I thrived to get you to open deep inside your heart to address those feelings that had evidently built up over the years.

I was fortunate enough to hear from you at one stage about how hurt you really felt inside. I have been given a chance to do the right thing. I will be forever grateful to you for that.

It is my God-given responsibility to show you how to love. I know I practice tough love a lot; that is one of the challenges I still need to overcome with God's love. I hope to strike a balance by way of this book.

It is my God-given responsibility to remind you of who you are, of what importance you are to me and to those whose paths you come to meet.

It is my God-given responsibility to guide you and show you right from wrong in the best way possible for I do not have an expiry date engraved on my forehead. I, too, will be called to my Creator and what good would I have been to you if I did not teach you any of the above.

I am not perfect, and I don't thrive to be. Instead, I thrive to be the person who tries to love with all her heart and never gives up on love.

I am so proud of you, my son, and I know that I have said it to you so many times, many a times not really getting into detail about why and how I can say that.

You are special in all ways and I am not just saying this because I am your mother.

Therefore…

But first, let me tell you a little about your father.

Nick and I

I met your father when I was 19 and he was 24. He had accomplished a lot in his young life. He had worked for a bank for a few years before I met him, but at that time, he had started a company with his friends and they seemed to be doing well.

Your father regarded himself as cool and he had this walk like he owned the place. He was confident, just like you.

He dressed well and his favourite brands for clothing were Seville Rowe, Levi's and Diesel. He wore the Black Jeans by Versace as his cologne and he went to the gym everyday besides the weekend.

I met him through his cousin, your Uncle Sydney's girlfriend, Chisenga, whom I shared a room with. Nick, as your dad was affectionately known to his friends, but born with the name Cornelious Tichakunda Maturure, came from a big family. He was the sixth born from a family of seven.

Godfrey Maturure was the first in his family. He was Vanessa's dad and he had passed away a few years before I met your dad. Uncle Kenny was the second, and then came Aunty Rati, Uncle Michael, Aunty Shami, then your dad and finally Aunt Tari.

Your grandparents had left their house in the city for their rural home in Shurugwi. Your dad, Aunt Tari and Uncle Kenny lived in the family house.

As you know, I grew up with my aunt, Mrs Reid, and lived with all my cousins: Lydia, Debra, Lucy, Rodney and Louise. Eventually, when my dad remarried my step-mum, I went to live with them, my step-sister, Gugu and step-brother, Mzi.

I moved out of home when I was eighteen. To be honest with you, I was bitter inside that my mother was absent. I did not understand why. It made my relationship with my step-mum very unsavoury.

So, fast forward to the following year, when I was nineteen and when I met your dad.

With music so loud, not just any music but Tupac, B.I.G and a few other artists, Nick would come to pick me up and he could be heard from a distance. I thought it was cool, which girl didn't. We went places and it just didn't matter where we went, he just loved to drive.

After my friend Chisenga immigrated to the United States, I moved in with my friend Iris. Iris and I had been friends since high school. Her mother had passed away and she had been the only child. She didn't want to live alone, so I went to live with her.

The following year, I planned a surprise 25th birthday party for Nick. I arranged with his friends without him knowing. It turned out so well and I don't remember when he stopped thanking me for that. I was due my annual leave soon after his birthday and we drove to meet Uncle Michael and his family who lived four hundred kilometres away. I modelled part-time and kept my job as a secretary. Nick continued his business with his friends. I decided to open my own modelling school which I called '*Model Contour*' and Nick supported me fully. He would arrange transport for the photo shoots and encouraged his friends to support the cake sales I held to raise money. Even when I doubted myself, he assured me that I would do well. I didn't run the school for long. It became a luxury that a lot of people could not afford. So, I closed it down, but I got contracts to hold pageants and that paid exceptionally well.

I asked Nick to be one of the judges in a pageant and told him that he could ask one of his friends to be the other judge as I needed two extra. I already had two more judges. He made a joke of it saying to his friend that they had been given permission to watch.

Everything was perfect between us and I found him to be considerate, caring and above all loving.

Nick had several friends. His best friend was Uncle TC. They had been in school together and did all those things that boys get up to together. He was also very close to Uncle Michael.

Always speaking his mind, he once told me that he felt I was the one who could make or break him, and all the time I thought he was the one able to do that with me.

I felt loved, no doubt. We spent a lot of weekends together and he would drive me to work after his morning gym sessions.

It really felt like the perfect dream. We went shopping and to the clubs, even if he didn't drink or smoke and was hopeless when it came to dancing. I remember one time we went to the opening of a new club and they played a song I liked. I found myself on the dance floor and he came along. Even if he couldn't dance to save his life, he didn't mind being embarrassed for me. I thought that was such a good memory.

All I had to do was choose the hairstyle I wanted and he paid for it.

I received bouquet after bouquet from him and that was a breath of fresh air.

The launch of the *Benson and Hedges* was a huge contract and only four ladies were sought for that role. It included flights to all destinations and 5-star hotel accommodations. Nick asked me if I wanted to do it and I remember saying to him that it was very hard to get in as much as I wanted. He said he would speak to some of his contacts.

After two weeks, I was on board along with three other ladies for the induction. I made more money in a week than I made in my job in a month. It was an experience of a lifetime. It was a six-week contract and we only worked on Weekends.

He taught me how to drive. Of course, there were days when we would not want to see each other because of the arguments that came with the driving lessons, but all of them were temporary. We always looked back and laughed about them.

I met Aunt Shami and her family on one of our globetrotting escapades. My cousin, Debra, had got married. She lived on the same street as Aunt Shami. So, on one of Nick's trips to see his parents, I went with him so I could stay at Debra's. I thought I would surprise her.

But I was the surprised one as she had travelled in the opposite direction. I still wanted to stay and spend the weekend with my nephews. So, Nick proceeded after he introduced me to Aunt Shami who was down the road.

He came to pick me up on Sunday evening. On our way, he stopped at a takeaway to get some food. He proceeded to the pharmacy and wondered what he was looking for. He took out this card as we sat in the car. It read, 'I'm sorry'. And in it he had written how sorry he was that I had missed my cousin. He was just so thoughtful.

Prior to my 21st birthday party that my parents were hosting for me, he had mentioned that he wanted us to take it to the next level. He wanted to go and meet my aunt as it was tradition. That was the way to propose.

At that stage, I had met all his siblings and was yet to meet his parents.

So, when we went to see my aunt, she advised that we wait till after the 21st birthday party, which was a few months away at that time.

The party was scheduled two weeks after my birthday. But Nick arranged that we went out with my friends for dinner on my birthday.

My 21st birthday party was a success. I got a Jacques' Farrell watch and Nokomis Cologne from Nick. Shortly after that, he arranged for me to meet his parents – nail biting experience.

They were so warm. At that point, he wanted to meet my aunt again to arrange for him to meet my parents and a date was set.

I had to go home that morning and wait for Nick and his family. It was the first phase. I remember how proud my father was of me. Even after I had moved out of home at eighteen, I had been able to look after myself till twenty-one and I was about to get married.

I felt so lucky and loved beyond measure.

So, Nick had to come back to my parents with the bride price and his uncle who had to be informed by letter, so we waited. I still carried on and lived with Iris and her boyfriend.

One afternoon, just after work, I felt a slight pain on my left-hand side abdomen. I didn't think much of it and carried on. But it became evident that something was wrong. So, I informed Nick. He picked me up and took me to the doctor.

Our Joy

When the doctor said, "You are pregnant," Nick's face slowly turned from worry to excitement. He was overjoyed. The timing was perfect as we had started with the bride price negotiations.

His uncle and other members of his family came and paid the bride price. Since I was pregnant at that stage, I had to go with him to his parents to tell them. I went with my aunt Bahle. We spent the weekend with them.

I was spoilt rotten. I got everything I wanted. This made it easier for me to be pregnant.

As I grew bigger, I decided to move in with my aunt Bahle. I was not allowed to live with Nick yet, as his parents had to come and ask my parents first. That, too, was tradition.

On the 14th June 1999 at about 2pm, I went in to the Doctor and was rushed to the hospital. I was in labour. Nick had to go back home to get my hospital bags. I rode in the ambulance to the hospital.

Nick came back later that day, but was told that I would give birth in the morning. So, he went back home.

I gave birth at 12:05am Tuesday, the 15th June 1999. You were so little. You only weighed 2.5kgs. I remember the midwife asking me if I had a name for you and I said I did. I was going to call you 'Mzingaye', meaning, 'our house is a home because of you'.

After a few hours of sleep, I called Nick to tell him the news. I could hear his excitement on the other side. He couldn't believe that I had given birth. After that, I said, "Come, meet your son."

He paused a bit as if in disbelief and he responded by saying, "I'm on my way."

I forgot to tell him about the hospital visiting hours. It seemed that it was after I hung up that he showed up.

Let me try and describe to you what his reaction was when he saw you. First, he walked in past all the nurses. I don't think he even saw them. He saw me and hugged me so tightly I said, "Congratulations! You are a father." He leaned over to hold you. In his eyes, I saw the look of pure love. I knew that he would be a changed man after that. You melted his heart. I realised one of my purposes in life, which was to bring the two of you together. What an honour it was for me to receive by God!

The nurses came in and told him to come back later but he was so reluctant to put you down.

I told him that he could come back later. He asked me if I needed anything and then left.

10am–11am was visiting hour. I was looking forward to seeing him back. In walked his friends, one after the other, the room filled with bouquets and cards. The nurses had to come and ask again about which one of them was the father. They were as excited as he was.

When Nick came, he asked me what I thought of the name Ngonidzashe. I hadn't told him about the name I told the midwife. So, I decided that I liked Ngonidzashe, which means the Grace of God. I felt that a name from him was best because of the way you truly brought joy in his heart.

He always stayed longer after the visiting times just looking at you and not saying anything. You were so beautiful. I caught myself doing that a lot as well.

During that time, my aunt and step-mum visited and gave me some help and taught me a few tricks with the breastfeeding, which was so painful.

Your aunts, Shami and Rati, also called everyday just to check that all was going well. There was so much love going on. I felt that your presence melted everyone's heart.

I was in hospital for three days and Nick came to pick me up. I still had to go to my aunt's house and wait for his side of the family to come and ask my family to allow you and me to live with him.

On our way, Nick asked me what I wanted. I remembered that I was not comfortable on the bed I used at my aunt's house, so I said I needed a new bed.

No doubt, the bed was delivered the next day. But Nick also mentioned that he had something else in mind for me.

When I was settled at my aunt's house, Nick's parents came to visit as well. They were so overjoyed to meet you. They sang and prayed for you. With them, they brought an extensive list of names. You were the first grandson and everyone wanted to name you. You had a total of four names by the time they left, all of them written down on a piece of paper.

Pelandaba

When you were three months old, we moved in with Nick in his family home in Pelandaba. It was the first time for us to live together. We had spent weekends together, but it was never official.

I suppose that is the stage you can call it traditionally married.

Soon after Nick bought me a car and said he wanted to show his appreciation for giving him a son. I was so excited that at least, I could drive around with my friends.

Like I said earlier, Nick lived with Aunt Rati and Uncle Kenny. Vanessa came to live with us as well. There was also a gardener called Solomon. He was a friendly character and called me Mrs Nick because his wife was called Mrs Solomon.

I was due to go back to work and I was so worried about leaving you. Nick could sense my worries and decided that instead of getting one helper, we would get two, one to mind you and the other to take care of the house. It sounded like an innovative idea. But when the day came for me to go back to work, I wished I could clone myself instead. It was hard for me to leave you for eight hours, but I wanted to work too. It is never an easy decision to make.

Life has its up and downs as is the norm in any marriage and I will not pretend that it was perfect.

Living in the family house that already had a lot of furniture, made it difficult for me to feel like I was part of it. But slowly, we started replacing the furniture according to our taste.

When we had arguments, Nick and I, it was always that I felt we should have moved out and got a place of our own.

But he was adamant that he was the youngest of the sons and his parents had bestowed upon him the responsibility of looking after the house since they had moved to the rural areas.

There was no wining for me, so I had to try and adjust. I did not like the fact that my neighbours were grandmothers and grandfathers whom I had nothing in common with. The worst thing was that I felt like I did not belong in the church.

Something that I find quite a challenge to a lot of churches, nowadays, is creating an environment where everyone who comes to worship and fellowship can find their place and feel comfortable and belong.

I was a young mother aged twenty-two and a wife. There were no ladies my age in the church who were married and were mothers. I did not belong with the youth; neither did I belong with the women's group for that was only comprised of the much older congregation.

Soon, I decided that I would worship in the church that was based in the city where there was a younger congregation. Nick went to church occasionally. Most of the times, I went with you and Vanessa.

Nick spoke about the kind of wedding he wanted to have. I was mostly just concerned about getting out of that neighbourhood and living in an apartment on our own.

He continued to do very well in his business with his friends. We continued travelling and seeing places with you. Sometimes, he just took you for a ride in his car, still with the loud Tupac, Notorious B.I.G music, your poor ears!

He would be gone in the day with you and before he would leave, he would say, "Babe! Hook my son up with some fine threads. We are going for a ride." Yes, he was comic as well.

He cherished you and he always said he was a proud father. He was a good one too. You had your very own camcorder before you could even crawl, and that did not last as I thought there was a need for other items that you could really make use of. So, the camcorder lasted for one day in the house.

On your first birthday, a party was arranged and the guests left at early hours of the following morning. It was a good party. The cleaning on the other hand was not.

Your grandparents, aunts and uncle visited every now and then and it was always good to see them.

Nick felt a pain in his leg at some stage. He visited the doctor who advised him to see a specialist. After that, he had to undergo an operation to draw the fluid built up in his knee due to a biking injury he had had during his teenage years. It was not a cause of concern as he was only in hospital for a day. Still, it meant he had to take it easy. I drove him around for the month. After his review, he was given the green light. He was back on track and back in the gym again.

Nick had a trip to Italy with one of his partners. It was the furthest he had ever travelled from home, and he had a rough estimate of when he would be back.

I missed him. When he rang to tell me that he had arrived safely, I could sense I was going to cry and I knew just how far away he was. We carried on communicating for three weeks. He always said that he kept going on because of the smile he felt I had when I was on the phone with him.

He was still away on my birthday. But that morning at work, I walked into a big bouquet of flowers with a note, 'I miss you and love you, happy birthday', from Nick. Thank God for Interflora.

That was the last bouquet I got from him.

It was good to have him back home and the wonderful gifts he brought back with him. He told me of how beautiful the place was and how he wanted us to go as a family. He imported a Jeep *Cherokee* and he loved it a lot. It had a leather interior, seat adjustment features and cruise control etc.

It needed a few repairs here and there, but in no time, it was on the road.

I still drove the *Pajero* that he had bought me and it, too, was working quite fine.

The beginning of 2001 saw Nick and his friends struggling a bit with their business.

Nick encouraged me to enrol in college. I always wanted to advance myself, so I took up an Executive Secretarial course.

I was never one to ask about the issues regarding their business. I believed that the less I knew the better, as I wanted us to focus on our family away from work.

I was working as a PA for a fast food chain and was paid very well. But still Nick did not want to move and at some point, I wanted to move out the house with just you. But I was so in love with him.

There were times when I clashed with Aunt Tari, as you can imagine two women in the same house. Uncle Kenny was fine. He just loved his drink and sold anything he could get his hands on, including some of our personal stuff.

Those that he was unable to sell, he would bring back and claim to have recovered them from the thieves who had stolen them.

There was never a dull day with him. He had a heart of gold and in as much as he loved his drink, he cared a lot about others as well.

He always begged us to babysit you. I was reluctant as he was always telling us that he would walk with you to his friend's houses. His friends were one of those that you would have been terrified of, if you had met them on your own.

I remember one day, he insisted that he was taking you and Vanessa just to get bread from the shops. Somehow, you were all gone for quite a while and I was getting worried.

On your return, Vanessa mentioned that you had been sitting on the benches whilst he went to buy some beer. Uncle Kenny was trying to convince Vanessa that she shouldn't tell me that detail. I was wondering what benches and she finally said, "In the beer hall." I was very angry, but thankfully that was what I used later to support my initial reluctance to allow him to take you for further walks.

He never asked again after that.

Beginning of the End

In April of 2001, I noticed that Nick had started losing a lot of weight. I was concerned for him. Nick wasn't the one to really talk about his business. But one day, he did ask to speak to me. So, after supper I sat down and he told me that he had invested a large amount of money into the mining shares that he and his friends shared. That investment, he told, could only yield profits in five years or more.

He had also been awarded a contract to source onions for pickling by a large vegetable franchise and he had asked one of his friends to go and buy the onions. It was a huge contract and the consignment was a truck load.

Unfortunately, because of the communication breakdown, his friend brought the wrong size of onions and they were turned down by the franchise. They tried to sell what they could. April was a hot month and they couldn't sell all of them before they went bad.

That contract was a lot of money and they lost it. I'm not sure what the value of the contract was. I asked him what he wanted to do.

We had to sell one of the cars and I decided that it would be better if it was mine that was sold. Nick told me that he had bought another car from his friend and business partner named Michael Takawira. But your Uncle Sydney was using it and we could get it back if I needed it. I told him that we could manage with one car and we did.

We didn't spend as much time together as when we used to spend when we had two cars. I would leave in the morning for work and he would leave for the gym. I went to aerobics class twice a week and I must say I wasn't a regular. Going back to using one car brought back those good memories of him coming to pick me up with the loud RnB music. It wasn't a bad idea after all to sell the other car.

On the other side, I slowly saw him withdrawing from his friends. He was quiet-natured but he began to be more reserved. His plans were not working and he found himself in debt.

In June, we celebrated your second birthday. We didn't have a party, just cake and a few friends.

I worried about him a lot. He would drive me to work and he would tell me that he just needed to take a break from going to the gym. It wasn't long that I found out he would, in fact, sleep the entire day and in some days, he wouldn't even eat.

His health was deteriorating and I told him that we should go to the doctor. He hated going to the doctor.

One day, when I came back from work, the helper told me that he had not left the bedroom since morning. Although, I had spoken to him during the day, he had not mentioned to me that he was not feeling well. He had dropped me off at work and went back home.

I immediately reached the phone to call for an ambulance. I remember how he begged me not to and said that he wanted to spend some time with me instead. I knew I couldn't allow that, especially when he wasn't eating.

I called one of his friends asking for advice and he suggested that he goes to hospital. So, I ignored Nick's suggestion and called the ambulance.

I had to inform my neighbours before the ambulance arrived so that they were not alarmed.

I remember the ride to the hospital. I had to go on my own as Aunt Tari was not back from work and we hardly saw Uncle Kenny. Mostly, he came home when we were all asleep and he would be sleeping when we left.

In the ambulance, I was made to fill in a consent form. It felt so terrifying to be in such a situation, with all the medical equipment and Nick lying on the stretcher bed. In the section for my age, I cannot forget how way too young I thought I was to be going through that. I was twenty-three and was going to be twenty-four in three months.

As soon as we got to the hospital, I had to call Aunt Tari, Shami, Rati and Uncle Michael who, then, relayed the message to your grandparents.

Aunt Tari came as soon as I called her. Aunt Rati and Shami arrived in the morning. Uncle Michael travelled on the weekend.

I had to go into work to ask for some time off from work. Luckily, I had very understanding managers and they told me to take as much time as I needed.

The whole time, they were conducting tests on Nick and when your grandparents came, they felt that the hospital was not doing all that was possible to get him well again.

They wanted to move him to a more secluded and private setting.

I had to keep going to work. But I stopped going to college as I couldn't afford the fees anymore and I didn't have time anymore, with hospital visits as well. By the end of the week, the whole family had come to live with us. Nick remained in hospital.

While I was at work one morning, I was called by the hospital to come and sign the discharge forms and his parents had decided to move him to a private hospital.

I had to go sign the documents and help with the transfer.

When I got to the hospital, Nick needed me to help him take a bath before being transferred. So, I accompanied him.

This was one of those days which I can never forget. He looked at me and all I saw was someone in extreme pain. I couldn't believe how frail he had become in such a short space of time. I wondered why I couldn't see it all the time when I was with him at home.

He said he wanted to apologise that he was not feeling well and that he worried about you and what would happen to you and me if he died. I begged him not to speak like that. Although, I wanted to shed a tear or two, but I wanted so much to be strong for him. He needed that.

Nick was the breadwinner not only in our family, but his whole family relied on him a lot. Financially, he was more stable and any financial need that they had, Nick took care of it. Sometimes, I think he shouldered way too much for everyone else. He never wanted to admit that he was in financial difficulty. I went in to work and got a loan. I showed him the money in cash and assured him that we would pull through, but it didn't change the way he felt. He felt that he should have been the one to take care of the situation he was in.

I honestly think that he thought that he had failed to accomplish what he wanted and in his mind, nothing anyone could say would change that. He was going through a lot and I felt as though I couldn't get through to him.

I had meetings with the doctor who attended to him. He was always helpful with updates and communication on his progress and suggestions.

He suggested that he should have a meningitis test and he suspected that he suffered from it.

Arrangements were made for it and the results came back negative.

Back home, your grandparents had moved back in and the environment started getting hostile.

One day, when I came back from work, I was told that they wanted to have a meeting. So, I went to sit with them after supper. Your grandfather said that I should stop using Nick's car as they needed it to go to the hospital.

As days went by, I was beginning to feel emotionally drained. I had to try and get a lift from Aunt Tari if I wanted to go to the hospital as Uncle Michael used Nick's car to take your grandparents. Sometimes, Tari would tell me that she had too many people to carry and she had no space.

I used the mini bus. I had no problem with that. The only problem was that there was no direct transport to the hospital. I had to take two buses and walk about 3km from the main road.

By the time I got to the hospital, they would sometimes be leaving and on occasions, I would be told that if I needed a lift, I would have to join them. Of course, it wouldn't have made any sense for me to spend 10mins with Nick, so I declined that offer each time it was made. Because I declined their offer, they made sure that the helper did not cook until I got home. They told me that they were waiting for me to cook as the daughter-in-law has to. Sometimes, it was 8pm by the time I got home and it was winter.

On days when I found the family in the hospital ward, they would all gather around his bed and left me with no choice but to wait to talk to Nick till they all left...

Unfortunately, they said a lot of untrue things to Nick and sometimes, it felt like I was wasting my time being there as he, too, would ignore me because of what he heard about me.

On one occasion, he told me that instead of me using the bus, I should call Uncle Sydney and tell him to give me the car he had lent him. It was a *Peugeot 405* which Nick had bought from Michael Takawira.

The following morning when I got to work, I called Uncle Sydney and he told me that he would bring the car. Instead, he called Uncle Michael and told him that he was wondering why I wanted the car that did not belong to me.

So, Uncle Michael went to Nick and told him that I wanted to take a car from Sydney without consulting anyone. He said that they suspected that I wanted to sell the car because I asked if he had the registration book.

When I went to visit Nick that evening, he told me that I should learn to trust his family and they are there to help me, so I should run everything by them, especially regarding the car. From what he said, I had a feeling that more was said, and the last thing I wanted was to add more stress on Nick. No wonder I hadn't even told him that I used the bus. I had always maintained that I offered the car to his parents because I could get a lift from one of my colleagues, who lived in the same area as the hospital.

I decided that I would leave the car with Sydney and not pursue it further.

I continued using the bus and on weekends I would carry you on my back and go with you to see him. Each time, I told him that I had got a lift from one of my colleagues. I lied because I didn't want the car issue to be brought up again.

My routine was work, hospital and home. Each night, I cried and played my favourite song, *Angingedwa* by Rebecca Malope. *Angingedwa* means, 'I am not alone.'

Sometimes, it felt as though the ground I was walking on was as thin as air.

My dad did visit on several occasions when he wasn't on his Council duties. He had retired as Lieutenant Colonel and was elected as Councillor.

My step-mum also came as often as she could, but with no car, it too was difficult for her to access the hospital. My aunt Mrs Reid came with me when I still had a car. I would pick her up, but she found it too far to travel 3km from the main road. I understood that. So, many a times, I was alone with the rest of Nick's family.

Your grandparents had been living with us since the time Nick was admitted at the beginning of July. It had been a month when they needed to go and keep an eye on their home. Uncle Michael was also going back to his family after Nick's birthday on 31st July 2001, when he turned 30 years old.

Debra, my cousin, was coming to visit for the weekend. So, I asked your grandmother if I could use the car to pick her up because she wanted to see Nick. I had told her that I would go to Mrs Reid's house in Thorngrove after work. As soon as I got to Mrs Reid's, your grandparents came with Aunt Tari and Uncle Michael to drop off the *Cherokee*. They also asked to take you and Vanessa with them. I didn't mind. So, I told them that I would spend the weekend with Debra and Mrs Reid and that I would be back home on Sunday.

So, we proceeded to the hospital and at closing time, which was 7pm, we headed back to Thorngrove.

In the morning, we went to church. Then, we went to the hospital to see Nick and later we went back. I proceeded home later that evening.

I heard your grandparents coming in the night and in the morning, I went to greet them.

I proceeded to work on the bus and after work went to the bus terminus to catch the bus to the hospital.

It seemed like a normal day. I met the family in the hospital and as usual, they were leaving because they had spent the entire day there. I stayed and carried along on my own.

I got home a little later than 8pm and of course, I had to finish off the cooking and serve them. After all the cleaning in the kitchen, I wished them good night. Prayers were said and I went to sleep. But they never seemed to go to sleep until very late, most of the times. They always held meetings.

On this day, I was still listening to Rebecca Malope and you had fallen asleep when I heard a knock on my door. I reduced the volume on the radio, which wasn't that loud, but I did so to try and listen well as I could hear loud voices as well.

I heard Mrs Reid's voice. I got up to open the door and Aunt Tari told me that your grandparents wanted to see me. I was surprised that Mrs Reid was in the living room. I knew she went to bed as early as 7pm. I wondered how she came or whom she came with. Somehow, she didn't seem very happy to be there. So, after I greeted her, I sat down next to her.

Present were, of course, your grandparents, Aunt Tari, Uncle Kenny and Aunt Shami. Your grandfather said that he had called Mrs Reid to discuss why I chose to sleep in her house on Saturday night instead of coming home. Mrs Reid explained that because her daughter, also my cousin, Debra had travelled to come and see Nick. Since they had said they were taking you and Vanessa with them to their rural home, there would have been no one else at home who needed me there. After all they had agreed on it prior.

Your grandfather insisted that I shouldn't have done so. Something I did not understand for they did not seem to mind when I said it to them.

Mrs Reid got angry and asked if indeed that is what they had woken her up from her home for. She asked them why they didn't tell me that they did not want me to spend the night at her place in the first place.

Your grandfather went on to say that she should have told me not to. He said that I seemed to take it lightly that Nick was in hospital and I could just decide to spend the night away from home.

At that point, I felt like crying as I thought of the number of times I felt alone with no one to talk to. Debra had travelled to be with me and made me feel like I wasn't alone and now my aunt had to pay for that. It seemed so unfair that it was a crime for me to spend time with my family.

In the end, Mrs Reid got up and told me to wake you up and pack my bags because she wanted us to go with her. I refused because I was so sure that that is what Nick's family wanted so that they could go to him and tell him that I had left. At that point, I knew that very well as I had been accused of so many other crimes, which I had brushed off and kept my focus on being there for Nick and for your grandparents, I think that was their last option.

In that moment, my mind raced back to those incidents; one, when I left the hospital, Nick had asked me to take his cell phone home so I could charge it. This was the day before the car was taken from me. I had placed the phone next to the gear stick and had intentions of charging it when I got to work in the morning. When the car keys were requested from me that morning, I never remembered that the phone was still in the car.

When your grandparents and Uncle Michael found it in the car and out of battery, they went and told my neighbours that I had been trying to block Nick from communicating with them.

Other accusations were that I never smiled like I used to. I did my best but it was hard seeing Nick deteriorating and they said that I did not take care of their house properly. It was something that was only raised after Nick was admitted in hospital.

Going back to the incident when they had gone to pick up my aunt in the middle of the night, Aunt Mrs Reid persisted that you and I leave with her and I still refused. As she walked, she told me never to come to her house again and that she would never ever come back to see me again because I chose to stay with people who clearly were trying to get rid of me.

Indeed, they were. I knew that. But I wanted to be there for Nick. I knew exactly that they would have told Nick that I walked out. I never liked to live in that house in the first place, but that was not the time to leave.

A part of me accepted that Nick might not make it, but there was that part of me that prayed every single night for God to give us another chance. I had promised to be a better wife and had held on to the plans we had together.

I wanted to stay for that reason and I had also reluctantly told myself that if Nick did not make it, I would have had a responsibility to tell you exactly how he departed from this earth. Certainly, a line that read: I left because the family didn't want me there wouldn't have demonstrated courage and perseverance and love on this page.

I made that decision to stay. It dawned on me that you were already in Mrs Reid's arms and they had gladly handed you over to her. I had to take you back and put you back in bed.

I cried every night, and in the morning, I was PA to the Regional Managing Director. I performed my duties exceptionally. I had supportive Managers who always offered me to take time off, but work kept me sane. It was a good diversion to the harsh realities I faced outside it.

Later in the hospital, I was surprised that Nick did not speak about it, meaning no one had told him. I never ever said anything bad about your grandparents to Nick. I was mainly concerned for him to get better than anything else.

Mrs Reid kept her word. She stopped coming to the hospital and home even when I went to beg her to come with me. She would state that she has never in her life being treated like that and refused to be in the same room with his family.

The Jeep *Cherokee* started giving problems. In one of the meetings, your grandparents decided that selling it would have been a good option.

I didn't mention it to Nick but waited to hear from him about what he wanted to do.

He was in a very poor condition and the doctor wanted to take another meningitis test.

Nick told me that the registration book for the Cherokee was in his office and that if I went to the office, his partners would give them to me. Instead, I asked that they left them in the reception area. I hardly saw any of them in the hospital I didn't want an awkward situation, because I didn't know their reasons for staying away.

Uncle TC came often. His sister worked in the same hospital where Nick was and she was always going the extra mile for him.

After I picked up the registration, I noticed that it was changed to Nick's name but he had not signed at the bottom.

I went to the hospital to show him the documents. He tried signing, but he had got so bad that he couldn't even hold a pen.

I went home and practiced his signature several times until I was confident and signed it.

I never told this to anyone.

I gave the documents to your grandparents and they started looking for a buyer. Uncle Michael was back at this stage.

Within a week, they had got a good offer for it. Nick, however, stated that he wanted the money to go into his account, something that they could not argue with.

The doctor gave me the signing powers by writing a letter to the Bank Manager.

That same week, Nick was diagnosed with meningitis. He had to start on the medication. Unfortunately, it had to be imported or someone had to go out of the country to buy it.

In one of the meetings, your grandparents told me to go to the bank and withdraw some money so that they could send someone to go and buy the medication.

It was a large withdrawal and I was ushered in the bank Manageress's office. She was a pleasant lady. She had a genuine smile. She wanted to know what the money was for and I told her that we needed to buy medication for Nick. She encouraged me and somehow spoke to me like she knew what I was going through. I longed for someone like her to talk to.

I felt good leaving the bank that day. She gave me her business card and told me that I could call her anytime.

I handed the money and the receipts to your grandparents later that evening.

Nick did start to get better. He would talk at lot and talk about how he wanted to travel with us when he got out of hospital. It was so good to see him like that. He would laugh and share his jokes. It was a refreshing feeling. He mentioned to me that he had lent the *Peugeot 405* to Uncle Sydney, but he had got involved in an accident with it. Instead of getting it fixed, he took his girlfriend on a holiday. He also mentioned that Uncle Sydney was not at fault and the other driver paid him for the damages because they both decided not to get the insurance companies involved.

He always defended Uncle Sydney and it came as a surprise to me that he said that about him.

So, I asked him what he wanted me to do with the car. He said I should arrange with Uncle Sydney to take it to a panel beater Nick knew and trusted.

So, I promised to do that. The following day, I called Uncle Sydney and told him what Nick had said. At that point, I told him that I knew about the payoff he got from the accident and what he did with the money so that he wouldn't tell your grandparents.

After great reluctance, he told me where he had taken the car. I got the number and rang the manager of the garage. He said that he could not release the car because it had been sold to a buyer who was going to collect it the following day. I was so shocked when I heard that.

I had only seen Uncle Sydney in hospital once ever since Nick was admitted.

So, I convinced the Manager not to sell the car as Sydney did not have a right to sell a car that did not belong to him.

When I went to see the car, it was in bad shape. The doors to the right were both damaged, but the engine was still good and it was moving.

I arranged with the panel beaters and drove the car to them. The Manager was a friend of Nicks', but I had not met him before.

He was to give me a quotation, but he said that Nick was a good friend of his and wouldn't charge much for it.

I was happy that the car was safe. I told Nick and he, too, was happy. Luckily, he didn't tell your grandparents and I didn't either.

After the medication ran out, it was time to go to the bank again. Although, those trips to the bank meant that Nick was not well enough to stop the medication. It brought sadness to me, but I also looked forward to meeting the Bank Manageress who always listened and always knew what to say to make feel better.

I went three more times after that. Each time, I felt lifted in spirit after leaving. For once, I forgot about the struggles I had to endure and laughed a little with someone who asked me how I was. That was such an important question. When Nick asked me how I was, I knew that I had to be strong for the both of us. I couldn't be honest with him, but with the Bank Manageress, I felt that I could tell her anything.

On days when I walked the 3km distance with tears in my eyes, thinking about the possibility of losing Nick, who was my knight in shining armour in all ways. He loved me even when I thought I didn't deserve to be loved. I had grown up feeling that if my own mother could abandon me and never look back, then who could love me.

My mother was in the same country as I, but she never ever came to visit me. Even when I gave birth to you, she never came. I really do not know why. But Nick came along and told me that he loved me so much that I was the one who could make or break him.

So, the thought of losing him saddened me a great deal. I prayed for a miracle for him.

I couldn't afford to run the home with my salary, especially with the number of visitors we had. So, the landline was disconnected. My cell phone was malfunctioned as well.

Most of the times, the screen went blurred or it wouldn't charge, so I stopped using it.

I always kept in touch with the doctor from my work phone. The hospital also had Aunt Tari's cell phone number in case of any emergency.

One day, during Nick's talkative days, he told me that there was a train that came in the night through the hospital and it stopped next to the entrance. Then, it proceeded. He explained it so vividly. It scared me a great deal before learning that the patient on the first bed from the door had passed away the night before Nick told me that.

When my dad came, I would hear him say to Nick that he needed just to concentrate on getting better and not worry about us.

My dad also spent some time with me when he came. He, too, was very worried and I knew that he was trying to be strong.

At the end of August, Nick said he was too tired of the hospital and wanted to spend some time at home. I was glad to hear that, but your grandparents said that they were invited to a wedding which they could not miss.

So, on the Friday the ambulance brought Nick home in the evening while the whole family left for the wedding. They took you with them as well. A nurse came in the morning to administer his medication. I was working half day and told the nurse to leave when I got back.

Nick had taken a turn for the worse and he was unable to talk. He just nodded or shook his head. I slept next to him and I could feel his body heat up like he was on fire. I knew something was not right.

Vanessa's mother had visited, and I asked to use her phone to call the doctor. Immediately, the doctor asked me to call the ambulance and he planned for the hospital to prepare a bed for him.

I did that and told Vanessa's mum to alert the neighbours so that they didn't get worried. But they were worried and they ran to come and see what was happening.

They couldn't comprehend that we were left with someone so ill and that the rest of the family had gone for a wedding and they were to be back on Sunday.

The ambulance arrived and little did I know that it was Nick's last time at home and in the ambulance.

As soon as we got to the hospital, the nurses took care of him and gave him something for his temperature. I insisted that I wanted to spend the night at the hospital but Uncle TC's sister told me that I needed to sleep and take care of you. So, I listened and in the morning, I went back.

I spent the whole of Sunday with Nick. At 7pm, the hospital staff urged me go home and get some rest. So, I called for a cab as public transport was scarce on Sunday nights.

Your grandparents and the rest of the family came in the early hours of Monday morning. Because I heard them coming in and we had told them that Nick was back in the hospital, I woke up to go greet them and explain to them what happened.

The following Tuesday, Nick was back to his talkative state and said that he felt fine and that all the pain had stopped. My hopes were up. He said that since we had only married the traditional way, he wanted us to get married as soon as he left the hospital.

Unfortunately, he said that in front of his family who were not very happy about that.

From then on, I was picked up from work to the hospital and back home. When I stayed to kiss Nick goodbye, I was questioned what I was saying to him. I wonder how I managed those times, but this is what I know; I had you to keep me going and I looked forward to coming back home to be with you even if it meant dealing with the unsavoury treatment from your grandparents. You were my light at the end of the tunnel.

09/09/2001

On Sunday, the 9th September 2001, as was the norm, I went to the church in town which started at 10am–12noon and after that I went to hospital and spent the day there.

Your grandparents and the rest of the family went to the local church with a late start of 11am, so they went to the hospital first.

It was normal for them to leave me at home for I took the bus anyway. But that morning, I wondered why Uncle Kenny was up so early. It seemed like everyone was going to the hospital that morning. I never thought anything of it. I was grateful that Uncle Kenny could make it as he seldom went to the hospital. I carried on with getting ready. I had kept only one helper because it became an expense even way before Nick got ill and you were getting older and I was coping.

You were in the bedroom with the helper and I was in the kitchen making breakfast. I heard a knock on the door and I went to open.

One of my neighbours and the granddaughter of my other neighbour stood in front of me in a strange way, which immediately turned to shock as I greeted them with a smile. The elderly lady asked me if I hadn't heard, and I asked her what. She said that Nick had passed away at 8:10am that morning.

My world came crushing down. I don't remember how I ended up on the floor, but I remember the helper coming to help me up with the help of the granddaughter from next door.

It wasn't long that your grandparents and the rest of the family came back, until such point I never thought of the time they came back. Nothing made sense as I thought he was getting better.

I don't remember when my step-mum and Mrs Reid came. Time seemed to just go by. All I could hear was noise and I wanted it to stop. I wondered what I would tell you.

It felt like my heart had been ripped from my chest. I felt I couldn't breathe. I needed to hear something to make this feeling go away.

I wanted someone to tell me that Nick was coming home and we would be a family again. We would have that big wedding he spoke about and go on the holiday he always talked about. I didn't understand it.

When I saw my step-mum, I could not even move. She came and hugged me and said how sorry she was. Mrs Reid was so devastated that she was crying so much more than I was.

Soon, there were people coming to offer their condolences and I was required to sit on a mattress with your grandmother, my step-mum and Mrs Reid.

I was surrounded by people who were not my age and I didn't know what to say to them.

Each time I heard your voice coming from wherever you were in the house, I felt like crying.

I just sat on this mattress and was hardly visible. I was petite and surrounded by women most of whom were old enough to be my grandmothers.

Even when my friends and colleagues came, they never sat with me. They expressed their condolences and disappeared into the kitchen. I couldn't leave the place where I sat as it is culture that you sit on a mattress the entire day and even sleep there.

There was to be a prayer in the evening and the church congregation attended.

In the morning of the 10th September 2001, Uncle Michael, Uncle Kenny and I don't remember who else called to talk to me. I went outside and they told me that they needed us to go to the bank to withdraw the rest of the money in Nick's bank account. They emphasised that I couldn't tell the Manageress that he had passed away as they would freeze the account until the estate had been round up. This was the only money there was to have a decent funeral for him.

Nick had medical insurance, but no life insurance.

So, I had to get ready and remove the black clothes that I had on and I wore something else. I had to apply a little makeup to try and conceal the puffed eyes from all the crying I had been doing the night before.

On the way, I was aware that I was going to lie to the same Bank Manageress who was my pillar of strength, the one person I would have loved to tell about my loss because I knew that she would have said something appropriate to make me feel better.

As I walked in to the bank, I had to compile myself. She came out to meet me and I forced a smile as she ushered me to her office. I told myself that I had to protect her. If I told her that Nick was in the mortuary, she would have had to deny me access to the funds because of the laws that govern deceased estate accounts and I know it would have bothered her to do that.

So, I had to keep it together. She was her usual cheerful self and wanted to find out why I was withdrawing all the money from the account. So, I had to lie to her and say that we were taking Nick out of the country for treatment.

Like always, she wanted to know if I was okay with it. I thank God for the strength he gave me to be able to leave that office without breaking down.

She wished me the best of luck and as I left she said that she knew that Nick would be fine and wanted an invitation to the wedding.

I thanked her and headed straight to the car. I went back home and changed into my black clothes.

That was the last time I saw the money.

So, while we went to the bank that Monday morning, Aunt Tari went looking for a Preacher to preach and the service which was planned for that evening before we left for Shurugwi, your grandparents' rural home.

Nick was scheduled to be buried on Tuesday, 11 September, 2001. So, we had to leave for Shurugwi on Monday night after the service.

Nick was carried in a coffin by his friends. I still could not believe it, that the same door he walked through a few months ago was the same door he was carried in by his friends, lifeless and never coming back. That is a constant memory in my mind.

The house was packed and I saw faces of people whom I hadn't seen in a very long time.

After the opening prayer, the preacher came forward and he introduced himself.

I knew him. I remembered him from High school. He was the Scripture Union Leader and led all combined Scripture Union meetings that were held with our neighbouring schools. He had been given the nickname of 'Pastor' and I was not surprised that he had become a preacher.

I was happy to see him as I thought that he probably could relate to me because of the age similarity and I was confident that he knew his Bible. I thought he would just say one verse that I would hold on to, use it to heal me and read to you as you grew older.

He finished the preaching without mentioning any of that. I felt emptier and disappointed. When he mentioned the people that Nick had left behind and mentioned a special verse and a prayer for them, I realised that he did not say anything about you or me.

Aunt Tari had not told him that you and I existed. No wonder she had called him because he was not from the area we lived. So, he wouldn't have known anything about the family other than what he was told.

I knew of two verses in the bible that would have brought comfort to me and in turn yourself. *Exodus 22:22-23*: "You shall not mistreat any widow or fatherless child. If you do mistreat them, and they cry out to me, I will surely hear their cry." *Psalm 68:5:* "Father of the fatherless and protector of the widows is God in His holy habitation."

I knew these verses and just wanted someone to echo them to me and expand on them as a way of reminding my in-laws that there was no need for further hostility. I feared what they would say and do next. I was tired of being quiet at that point. I just wanted time to mourn Nick and to be strong for you.

Soon after that, it was time for body viewing. According to norm, friends and everyone else viewed first.

After that, it was my turn, my step-mum helped me up and as I got closer, I couldn't move further. I didn't want to accept that that was it. I had to say goodbye to my first love, the man who taught me how to drive, my mentor, my best friend and your father. "How about all the plans we had," I asked myself. It didn't seem fair at all. I felt robbed. I kept screaming, "No Mama, no Mama, no."

I had to be strong. My step-mum begged me repeatedly to go and say goodbye to him. I moved closer and looked at him. He really looked dead. His face was pale and when I leaned over to kiss his forehead, I couldn't believe how cold he was.

He really didn't look like he was coming back. Nick was gone and gone for good.

As I went back to sit down, the Preacher came to ask my step-mum who I was. She told him that I was his wife and you were his son. He said a prayer for you and me, but I really did not hear any word of it. There was singing going on in the background. Soon, we were saying 'Amen' and getting ready to leave for Shurugwi.

It must have been 10pm when we left. I can never forget the way my step-mum never left my side. I had a bad relationship with her which is the reason I moved out of home when I was eighteen.

She was my pillar of strength and I remember how she shouted at Uncle Kenny after he told the helper to stay behind so that she could watch over the house. She asked him how I would have been able to mind you when I still needed to deal with losing Nick.

She said they would have to get someone else to mind the house. You were way too young to know what was going on and I remember promising myself that I should tell you exactly what happened when you are old enough to understand. I asked my step-mum about when I should tell you. She said I should whisper in your ears as you slept; at least that way, you would know even if you didn't understand.

We arrived in Shurugwi in the early hours of Tuesday morning. My colleagues came all the way as well and the burial took place at 10am.

The Aftermath

September 11, 2001: That is the day your dad was laid to rest and the same day, America experienced an event that will forever be remembered because of the number of lives lost when Osama Bin Laden orchestrated the bombing on the twin towers. I have no recollection as to how many lives were lost that day. What I know is that a part of me died as well that day.

I couldn't be the same person.

My father could not attend the burial as it was in short notice. On our way back from Shurugwi, we went to drop off Mrs Reid and met my father there. He had arrived on the same day we left for the burial, but could not follow us as he did not know the way. It was good to see him even though he was speechless and heartbroken.

I went back to work after a week. I couldn't stay at home. I had to prepare for the ceremony where they distributed your dad's entire possession and a date had been sent. I informed my parents.

Only Mrs Reid and my dad could attend on the day and a few of your grandparent's relatives, Aunt Tari, Uncle Kenny and your grandparents.

I had to bring out your dad's entire items of clothing and shoes. Everyone was supposed to choose something. Mrs Reid and Dad didn't want anything as they felt that you should be the one to get most of his belongings. Your grandparents and their relatives shared the items amongst themselves. You were given a pair of shoes. I did not object to anything and only took the last watch he wore. It was a citizen watch and I needed that just as a reminder of the time we had spent together.

I mentioned that I wished to move out of your grandparent's home. I felt that your dad was no longer there. I really did not see the need for me to stay.

It came as a shock that your grandparents objected to that as they had made sure that I felt unwanted before your dad passed away.

They wanted me to stay for another year. I objected to that and went against their will. I moved out on the first week of October, 2011.

I was told prior to moving out that I could only move out with my clothes and nothing else that your dad and I had bought together. I had no problem with that.

I was also told that I was not to have access to the *Peugeot 405* that I had taken to the garage. I didn't have a problem with that either.

I was told that I should leave you with them and they said that I couldn't afford to take care of you the way they could. That I did not agree with. I told them that there was no way that could happen.

Not after the way they had treated me and certainly not after my mother had walked away from me and left me with a feeling of inadequacy was I going to put you through that.

I planned to move out and made sure that Uncle Kenny was at home when I took my belongings. We moved in with Mrs Reid and your cousins, Lexy and Dumi.

It felt good to leave that house, but is was sad too that I had shared some good memories with Nick in the same house.

I turned twenty-four on 14th October, 2001 and I bought a cake that I shared with everyone at home. I missed the bouquets from your dad and the wonderful presents.

You and I shared a bed with Mrs Reid. I remember that one morning Mrs Reid asked me how I couldn't hear you calling me because you needed to go to the bathroom. She was amazed that I could sleep like a baby after all I had been through.

I was so glad to hear her say that because it gave me a chance to explain to her why I didn't want to go with her when your grandparents made me feel unwanted.

I told her that it was important for me to be there until the end and I needed to be able to sleep better without any regrets. Today, I can say that if the love I had for your dad could have saved him, he would still be here. But unfortunately, it was his time.

At work, the ladies were always concerned for me that I was always at home and never going anywhere. I really didn't feel like going anywhere. On 30th October, one of my colleague's relative was getting married and she begged me to come along, just to get a bit of air. I agreed just to get her off my back.

It was a Saturday and the wedding was beautiful. Soon after we arrived, I saw Uncle TC's sister who worked at the hospital where your dad was a patient.

I thought she would be happy to see me, but she had a very concerned look on her face. We exchanged pleasantries and then she asked me why I didn't come to the hospital on 9th September 2011. I remembered that day, so I was still explaining to her that I got the news of your dad's passing before I left the house to go to church.

She interrupted me and said that she had personally called Aunt Tari on her cell phone and told her that your dad had to be put on oxygen. The doctor had requested that the family go to the hospital immediately. At that point, my mouth went dry. My heart started beating so fast that I had to sit down. She went on to say that the doctor had asked me to meet him there.

She took a deep breath when she said that the family was asked upon their arrival, where you and I were. Your grandfather said that I was not in their tribe.

Since I was born, I don't remember a time when I was that angry. To think that I was deprived of the chance to say goodbye to your dad, after all that I had endured from his family, because I wanted to be there till the end.

I wondered what Nick thought when he didn't see either me or you. What I would have given to be in that room that day, to see him hold you for the last time. Maybe he had something to say. All those thoughts raced on my mind.

I needed to leave the wedding. My intentions were to go to your grandparent's house and break every window and anything that stood in my way.

My friends talked me out of it. I had to calm down and not interrupt the wedding. I convinced my friends that I wouldn't do anything stupid, but I needed to go home.

I lost the little respect I had left for your grandparents. I decided that I would fight for the *Peugeot 405*, just to get on their nerves.

I never told anyone about this for a long time. I didn't want to tell Mrs Reid and get her worried.

Give Me Strength

On Monday, I decided that I needed to let out some steam after work. I went to the movie house and watched a movie that I don't even remember. I needed to gain some time so that I when I decided to go home, it was dark enough for people not to see my tears. I cried buckets all the way from town to home. I never worried about anyone noticing when I got home as the lights were very dim and Mrs Reid went to bed early. I washed my face and had my supper. Then, it was straight to bed.

At that point, I had hired a helper to assist with the chores and she was excellent.

I continued with my movie routine and it seemed to work as I had not had a chance to mourn your dad.

I sometimes wondered where his friends had disappeared to. Even my friends disappeared. I never asked them. I just figured that it was because they didn't know what to say to me.

Uncle TC had lost his wife a few years back and I didn't want to burden him. I knew that the few times I met him in town; he was heartbroken about the loss of his friend. Mrs Reid always talked about how much he cried at your dad's funeral.

There was a lady who worked at the passport office and had asked her to help me apply for a passport for you. She was related to your grandparents and her husband was a business partner with your dad.

I went to find out from her if it was still okay to get her assistance in applying for your passport. She told me that she was told not to have anything to do with me and your grandparents were handling anything pertaining to you. I didn't understand what she meant, but I didn't want to nag her.

A few months later, whilst in my office, I received a call from the receptionist from work. There was someone to see me.

I went downstairs and I found one of your grandparent's relative. She had been asked to come and call me by your grandparents. They were across the road at the government offices where they register births and deaths.

I agreed to go with her. There I met your grandparents. It was the first time for me to meet them after finding out how they deliberately didn't tell me that your dad was dying even after the doctor had instructed Aunt Tari to tell me.

I was not angry anymore. I just did not have respect for them. I greeted them and waited our turn on the counter. There was just one more person.

Your grandfather had an A4 brown envelope which he seemed to guard so much. So, I asked him if I could see what was in it. He replied by saying that they were just the documents from the hospital to enable us to get the death certificate for your dad.

I wasn't that stupid to believe it. So, I grabbed the envelope from him and went through it. Everyone was shocked and in my heart I was saying, "I bet you didn't think I could do that, right?"

I found an affidavit which read that your grandparents were looking after you and that they did not know where I was and that they had tried countless times to look for me, but I had left you with them and they couldn't find me.

After reading that, I turned to him and this is what I said to him, "You have the nerve to lie on an official document that is certified by law about my whereabouts. You have not seen your grandson since I moved out and yet you know where I live. Today, your relative came to call me, just across the road from this office and you say you don't know where I am. You must be joking." At that point, everyone in the building had come to gather around. I was so bold and really did not care. I had nothing else to lose.

Our turn came and we went to the counter. The lady asked us what the noise was about and I showed her the affidavit. She, then, said that she had refused to take the document and the same document had been rejected twice before by the same office. It did not make sense that they could not find me.

They did not have a choice that day but to find me. The lady asked me to sign for the death certificate and she asked me if I wanted to keep it.

Usually, a death certificate is given to the person responsible for the estate of the deceased, i.e. his possessions, his money and his debts. I had none of those and I was not allowed near them. It was of no use for me and we were not married in the court. I would have had to get witnesses that we were indeed married and I didn't want to go through all that. I wanted to focus on providing for you and keeping my job. Taking your grandparents to court for your father's estate was going to be an arduous process, not to mention, time consuming.

I had been through enough. I gave them the certificate and wished them well.

I went back to work and carried on as usual. I got another call from the receptionist. I had another visitor. It was Aunt Tari. They had been instructed by the officials in the government buildings to give me the documents.

Amongst the affidavit and the death certificate was your birth certificate as well. I didn't know that they had it.

Aunt Tari was so uncomfortable that she couldn't even look at me. I told her that I needed to get back to work. So, she left.

When Days Are Dark...

Weeks went by and I eventually found a flat in town. So, you and I moved into it. The helper came along to be with you when I went to work. Faro, your cousin also came to live with us.

I decided that I would proceed with getting the *Peugeot 405* fixed. I knew that your dad would have wanted that. I encountered a lot of problems with that. No one was willing to help me, especially Uncle Sydney and Michael Takawira, as the ownership of that car was still in his name.

All he needed to do was to change the ownership so that I could sell the car easily. But he always told me that he was busy, or simply ignored my calls.

I managed to get the car repaired but the ownership was still a pain. I sold it without the change of ownership and wrote an affidavit to support what had happened. The new owners were happy with that until they decided that it was not good enough.

They reported me to the police station for selling a car that did not belong to me. The policeman came and picked me up from my work place. He took me to the police station. Even after all that, Michael Takawira wouldn't help. I spent a few hours in the cell and I had to agree to settle for half the money the new owners owed me. In other words, they got the car for next to nothing. I had to agree to that for them to drop the charges.

I was released and at that moment, I felt I needed to get away and go somewhere far from all that.

One day, I got a call. It was a gentleman with an Italian accent. He introduced himself as Koullouros and he said that he worked with your dad. He wanted to meet with me to discuss a few things. He told me where he worked, so I went to meet him after work.

I had never seen or heard of him before. He said that he wanted to help me and you financially as he knew that it was tough since your dad was gone.

I was amazed that he looked for me to offer help and yet the people I had expected to help me were nowhere to be seen. I had tried countless times to get in touch with Uncle Sydney for him to help me buy the doors for the *Peugeot 405*, but he had been avoiding my calls so much that I gave up.

Koullouros was of much assistance as he always gave me monthly allowance that enabled me to enrol you in Pre-School. I could afford a lot of other things.

I had made up my mind that I wanted to leave the country. I told Kollourous that I would keep in touch.

I wanted a better life for me and you and I didn't want to depend on him as he had a family of his own. That is how I left Zimbabwe.

Kyriakos Koullouros and his family

A Bit of History...

Just to rewind a bit from the page before I began telling you about your dad.

I lived with my grandparents, my mum and her siblings since birth. We lived in a remote rural area where the sight of vehicles was the highlight of any day.

My dad was in the military and after the liberation struggle for Zimbabwe's Independence, he came to visit me. I was five years old.

I remember walking towards him, but I don't remember whom I was with. It was the first day that I met him. He introduced himself to me as my dad and I nodded in agreement, simply because I didn't know what to say.

We boarded a bus, just me and him. I remember how excited I was as I had a lot of bragging to do when I got back home to my friends, about being on a bus, or so I thought...!

I made sure that I kept a photographic memory of everything I saw from looking outside the window.

The journey eventually wore me out and I fell asleep. My dad woke me up when we reached our destination. When I opened my eyes, I thought we would be back home, but we had arrived in the city.

I was terrified because my friends always thought that all the people in the city spoke English and I had no clue of it.

We got off the bus and got in a car. I was so alert because I was restless, and I didn't know how to ask when I was going back home.

We eventually arrived at a house that was built out of concrete bricks. There was a row of these houses, but a few of them had been plastered and painted to look beautiful. I was the first one from my family to see such a house. My grandparents' huts were made up of mud and were thatched.

My dad introduced me to four children; Lydia was the eldest, Debra was the second, Lucy came third and then came Rodney. Their mother was my dad's sister, my aunt, Mrs Reid, who lived with her husband.

I was welcomed to the house, but I still wanted to know when I was going home. I don't remember anyone explaining to me that I was not going to go back home, neither did I get the memo.

I was hoping that someday my mother would come and take me back to my grandparents' home. I would wait at the gate sometimes, just hoping that someone would come.

My dad did not live in the same city as Mrs Reid, so he was gone a few days after our arrival. Still, I hoped that someone would come and take me back home. Eventually, the clothes I had brought with me got smaller and tore.

I had my cousins to play with, but we were so poor that I felt embarrassed to go out and play with other children. They seemed to look very well taken care of.

Sometimes, my aunt and uncle would fight and my cousins would encourage me to take sides by pulling the parent they favoured on that day.

It was a traumatic experience for me because I had never experienced that. At times, my uncle would come late at night and wake us all up to give us sweets. That was good, but not after it was followed by the fighting.

One day, my uncle brought us all chewing gum and woke us up to give it to us. In the morning, I had a lot of it in my hair.

I couldn't get it out, so I had to ask one of my cousins to cut it out of my hair.

Those are the few lighter moments I remember from that time in my life.

I looked forward to going to bed every night as I had the freedom to dream about the kind of life I wanted for myself. I would let my imagination run wild. I always knew that I wanted to be successful.

The mornings were a drag. My cousins and I slept in the living room floor. In the morning, we had to get up, fold all the blankets and put them away.

I thought of a plan one day and decided to ask our neighbour for a sewing needle and some thread so I could try and mend my clothes.

I knew that she probably had all the colours of sewing threads there were. They were well off. She was a housewife and had three grown children. Only the last of her children and her granddaughter lived with her. Her husband had a decent job.

Every morning, the milk man delivered milk to their door. I envied that because back at my grandmother's village, we milked goats every morning and we could drink as much milk as we wanted.

There was no such luxury in the new house. My aunt and uncle struggled to put food on the table and milk was certainly one of things last on their grocery list.

I gathered enough courage and went knocking on their door. The lady, Mrs Ngonyama answered the door. I told her that I had been sent by my aunt to ask for a needle and thread.

I could tell that she had her doubts. My aunt was the last person on earth to sit and mend clothes. She often left the house at midday and didn't return till the night.

There was no structure. My older cousins, Lydia and Debra took it upon themselves to ensure that we came back home at a reasonable time after playing.

My aunt drank a lot, but I don't know if I could call her an alcoholic. There was no way that she could have the time to sit and mend clothes.

Reluctantly, my neighbour gave me the sewing needle and thread. I remembered watching my grandmother sewing. So, I knew how to thread a needle.

I started working on my torn clothes and in no time, I was done. I returned the needle and thread back to my neighbour.

I gained a bit of confidence to go out and play with the other children after that. As the clothes were getting smaller, not even the thread I had used to patch them up could stop them from tearing up again.

I went back to my neighbour one more time and was surprised that she didn't seem to mind. But she warned me to be careful with the needle as it was dangerous.

I remember the few different times that my dad would visit. We seemed to have more meals and we would go shopping for clothes. It was always an enjoyable experience.

We didn't have a television. We went to one of our neighbours to watch a black and white television that they had in their lounge.

One evening, after watching TV at the neighbours', I felt tired and decided to go home to sleep. When I arrived at home, I found my aunt and dad discussing my new name.

As I walked in, my dad said, "You are right on time. Your aunt and I were discussing a new name for you since you will be starting school soon."

I knew, then, that I wasn't going back to my mother and my grandparents. I sat down and listened to them come up with names. Eventually, I was given the name, 'Alexia'.

It seemed hard for me to say it. My dad said that I had to make sure that the whole family gets used to my new name and encourage my friends to get used it too.

I went to bed that day thinking of what a challenge it would be.

In the morning, I had forgotten what the new name was. So, I went to ask my aunt, but she, too, had forgotten. So, we had to wait for my dad to wake up.

Eventually, he did and he wrote it down. I went to my cousins and announced that I had a new name and it was Alexia.

They all stopped and starred at me. It was like saying my name is 'Cher' in present day.

Of course, they asked me to repeat what I had said and I said it again. They were surprised that I could say one word in English. They couldn't help laughing. They just felt that the name was too posh for someone from a village.

It didn't seem long after that. I was on the bus again with my dad, but this time to get a new birth certificate.

I was due to start school the following year, the year when I turned six years old.

During that wait, my uncle left home and never returned until this day. First, I heard my aunt talk to the neighbours and tell them that he would be back.

Eventually, my aunt sold all his clothes.

The day came when I had to begin Kindergarten. I was enrolled in a multi-racial school. I was excited that I was going to school just like any other child my age.

I couldn't sleep the night before. I had my lunch packed and uniforms arranged so that in the morning, I wouldn't delay.

Two of my cousins went to the same school although they were in higher grades.

I had no idea what the classroom was going to look like or what I was going to learn, but I was ready to go and see.

It was a far enough distance that we had to walk. Eventually, we got to the school and my cousins took me to my classroom.

My worst fears came true. My teacher was White! I wanted to jump from a ship. I knew, then, that the whole arrangement wouldn't work at all.

Most of the pupils in the class were white and a few were Indians. I don't remember how many black pupils there were.

When the teacher stood in front of the class and introduced herself, she went straight into talking. It wouldn't have made a difference if I had requested ear plugs. I watched her lips move, but I could make no sense of what she was saying. Talk about being thrown into the deep end.

I knew then that it was a disaster as she obviously couldn't understand *isiNdebele,* which was the only language I was so fluent in.

Every day was the same, but I noticed a pattern. At some stage during the day, she would get out plastic table cloths and lay them on our desks. That meant it was lunch time. I didn't need English translation for that. It also meant that after eating, we could go and play outside.

The class sang songs courtly and I wondered where and when had they all learnt them. I started feeling as if I was so behind. I never knew then that most them had gone through Pre-School prior to kindergarten.

This went on for the entire year. I don't remember any day being different.

Things at home were different though. My aunt had given birth to the last of her five children. She was a girl whom they named, Louise.

It was a good feeling to have a baby in the house. It wasn't long until my aunt was back to her routine though. Mostly when we got back from school, she would leave the house to go to her friends' or the neighbour's house.

Two years later we moved houses, it was still in the same neighbourhood. Again, no memorandum was sent. I just found myself packing. I was a bit sad because it meant that I was moving away from the Ngonyama's. I enjoyed watching the milk man's early routine of delivering milk to their door. It just seemed so posh. I wanted to grow up to be able to have that service. Till then, the Ngonyama's had played a huge part in enhancing my imagination. Each time they were visited by people, who dressed well and drove beautiful cars, I would incorporate that visual into my imagination time before I went to bed. The only difference is that I would be the one driving the beautiful cars and wearing the beautiful clothes.

The house we moved into was the same size as the one we had lived in. Although, the previous house faced the hospital, the new neighbourhood had houses built facing each other. This made it seem like we were surrounded by people.

Financially, things took a turn for the worst. There were days when we went without food. Sometimes, we had pap sugar and water.

My aunt got different tenants all the time to occupy one of the two bedrooms in the house. It meant that the seven of us shared one bedroom.

At one time, I remember that she got tenants to occupy the two bedrooms and the living room. It meant that we slept in the kitchen floor. Those are the situations that disturbed me and really got me thinking about what I wanted for my life. I knew that I did not want to live like that or put my children through that.

In the mornings before school, we would wake up and knock on the door for the tenants in the living room to open the door so that we could use the bathroom. In the night when nature called, we used the toilet that was built outside.

We had days when the school would engage the parents and pupils in fundraising activities. It entailed all pupils to wear civilian clothing and donate a small fee to the school project.

I hated those days. I never had any money to give and had no decent clothes to wear. I had one dress apart from my uniform. I don't remember where I had got it from. It had a zip at the back. It was pink in colour with no sleeves, had a bodice and a flared skirt attached. Somewhere along the lines, the zip malfunctioned and I had to improvise. So, I sewed it closed from the bottom and left enough allowance to be able to fit my head in when I wore it. I wore my school shoes with the dress and yes, I looked awful and I knew it.

In the school, there were some children who looked so loved and well taken care of. They were always presentable and clean. It was a good feeling to see them as it was material for my imagination time too.

I don't remember making friends in the school, but my cousins were in the same school, except Lydia, who was the oldest. She went to a school that was not too far from home and we had a long distance to walk to the school.

Four years later, my dad asked my aunt to allow me and Debra to move in with him in an apartment in town.

It meant better care, food and more space – a bedroom with a double bed to ourselves. I don't remember feeling excited about that at all. I was accustomed to the life we lived with my aunt and feared the unknown.

My dad still worked out of town which meant we stayed alone during the week and saw him on some weekends.

Debra and I got used to it. Not long after that, my dad invited another cousin of mine to live with us. He was Debra's half-brother, Sebastian. He was not fun at all. We felt like we were watched by him all the time.

He ensured that we knew that he was in charge. He had a song that he loved and each time he played it, he would chase us away from the living room. He would dance to it until he was drenched in sweat. We thought that was so weird. There were times when he was good and helped us with our homework. Debra was in her second year of high school at that time.

Debra and I took a keen interest in church and attended the 'Family of God Pentecostal' church.

We attended every Sunday religiously. Although, I did not get why there was a need to pray every minute for different things, I only had one prayer which I repeated when I heard the words 'pray, pray, pray'. I prayed for a beautiful dress and a beautiful pair of shoes. That was all I wanted.

When it was time to attend Sunday school, there was always this little girl. I think she was my age. She wore the prettiest colours and finest clothing. Her hair was always done up so neatly. One word to describe her is 'angelic'.

Sebastian decided to start a new life in South Africa and my dad helped him to get all he needed for his journey. After my dad took him to the bus station, he too had to leave for his job.

We were home alone yet again. We celebrated our independence by filling the bath tub with a lot of water and dissolving a tablet of soap to try and create bubbles; we had no bubble bath.

My dad introduced us to my step-mum that same year. She brought structure into our lives. She was firm and unlike my aunt, who left us alone from morning till late at night and would need our help to get her bed done at times when she was too drunk to find her way. My step-mum never drank. She was a primary school teacher. She had two children, Gugu and Muzi. Gugu was a year younger than me and Muzi was five years younger than I was.

It did not seem like it was long after my step-mum and her children moved in with us that we got news from my aunt that Lydia had had a baby. She was still in primary school. I had no idea about how old she was, but she was way too young to have a baby.

Debra and I went to visit her. My aunt had moved the family to the living room to accommodate the new baby. Lydia and the baby had a bed to sleep on whilst the rest of the family slept on the floor. It was only then that I realised how lucky Debra and I had been to have moved in with my dad.

My step-mum had tried in all her might to get us to live a normal life which meant we had lunch boxes to take to school, three good meals a day and a toothbrush… Finally!

The father to Lydia's baby was a school teacher in the school attended and he agreed to support her and the baby. I wonder why he was not arrested. I am sure she was underage. Several issues were left for the family to handle. Back in the days, a lot of families chose to be silent about most, if not all of them.

We stayed the night at my aunt's place and in the morning, we went outside to play. The neighbourhood was decorated by several senior citizens, who felt lucky to be surrounded by energetic young beings because it meant that they could send us to the stores or to do anything else they felt were not able to do.

Each time I volunteered to do errands for them, they would reward me with the change which I took to my aunt because I thought that eventually she, too, would improve her life and be like the rest of the people who didn't have to give up so much space in their homes just to survive. That is something that I could not comprehend.

Back home, my dad and step-mum were planning their wedding. I had heard that my grandmother i.e. my dad's mother, would come for the wedding and I wondered if they would invite my grandmother, my mother's mother and my mother too. They lived in the same region with about 15miles apart from each other.

It was a small wedding that took place in the apartment. Both my mother and her mother didn't come and sadness covered my face.

I didn't enjoy the wedding.

From that point on, I began to wonder what life would have been like if I had stayed with them in the village.

It wasn't long after that, that my dad decided that I should visit them. It was exactly five years after I had left.

There were school holidays and both my dad and step-mum took me to the bus where we met up with Aunt Mrs Reid. She was also thrilled to go and visit them.

After Mrs Reid and I arrived at my grandparent's place where she and my dad grew up, I was accompanied to my mother's place by one of my cousins. We walked and it seemed like eternity.

Somehow, I didn't feel the excitement I thought I would feel when I went back. Maybe it was because I felt that I should have been told from the onset that I was going to live with my aunt. The years I had spent wondering when I would go back had left me feeling like I didn't want to go back to visit them, but to try and get answers.

We eventually arrived and I noticed a few things that I remembered from before I left. My grandparents were so excited and my cousins seemed to have grown.

We went into the kitchen and I was asked a lot of questions about my new school and my friends. I wondered all the time where my mother was. But I knew well not to avoid the questions from my grandparents and wait until the interview was over.

My grandmother mentioned that my mother was married and had moved to her new home. She also had two other children-girls.

One of my cousins was sent to notify her that I had come.

A few hours later, I could see her walking towards my grandparents' home. I had mixed feelings about her. I know I wasn't happy in the inside. I didn't know how to feel.

I have memories of the times when I wondered how life would have been like if she were in my life. It has been five years with no letter or any communication with her.

I wondered in my heart about how she felt and whether she missed me as much as I did or if she lay awake at night missing me like I had.

She entered the kitchen and seemed excited to see me; I am not sure if I reciprocated the same feelings towards her.

She sat down and asked me a lot of questions as well. My heart sinks at the thought of saying this, but I did not feel a connection to her at all. Maybe it was the anger in me. I could not let it out because it was not permissible for children to disrespect elders, no matter how unfair they felt; they had to handle the situation. Who was I to say anything? I just did as I was told.

After what seemed like a few hours, my mother mentioned that she had to go back to her family. I am struggling with this as I write it. I hadn't seen her in five years and all I get is 'a few hours'.

I wanted to break down and had questions as to what I had done to her for her to not care. Was I really her child? I asked myself.

That night when I went to bed, I shed a few tears. I felt that my dad had married and was happy and so had she. I felt that I didn't belong with either of them.

I suppose, I was just supposed to be happy for them both and leave it at that.

I went back home after a few days, and my mother came back to say goodbye on the day that I was leaving.

I went back twice after that. The second time, I was in third year of high school and the last time was after Nick had passed away.

There are a lot of things I ask myself about my mother and my relationship with her. Growing up, I couldn't comprehend why she never tried to communicate with me or even visit me.

I wanted to ease my own pain that was caused by her unwillingness to demonstrate motherly love. So, I told myself that I wouldn't judge her. Instead, I decided to create my own reason as to why she had let me go. For years, I believed that it was because she wanted me to get a good education away from the village where the height of life was getting married and having a sizable number of children.

However, it bothered me that she was still absent from my life. There were things that I felt inside that she will never know of, especially when I went through challenging times.

She was never there. Nick passed away in hospital after he had spent almost three months and not one day did she visit, she didn't attend his funeral.

I visited her with you and Mrs Reid before I left for South Africa to tell her that I was leaving the country.

I tried communicating with her several times, and all those times, she complained that I did not support her financially. I called to ask her what she wanted. I bought her the items she wanted, including a phone, before I left from South Africa to Ireland.

All I could say is that even if I tried to justify her actions regarding letting me go, I was still not satisfied about how she could turn her back and never look back. More so after I had you, there is and never will be a situation that will make me choose to abandon you, no matter how old you are. It is a painful feeling and I do not wish it upon anyone.

There were times when things had been tough and finances were tight. As a mother, I have had to go without fulfilling my needs so that you could have what you need.

I feel that it is my duty as a mother to ensure that I provide sufficiently. Not in monetary form only, but emotionally and socially as well.

The absence of my mother in my life has given me a template of the kind of mother I do not want to be. I thank her for that.

I just hope that she will be able to make it to my funeral. I know that I will visit her when we visit home and still give her what she requests, if I have the finances to do so.

Family

When we came to Ireland, we left all our family behind. That was hard, especially not knowing when we were ever going to see them again.

We have found new family here in Ireland though. You have made friends that are as close as can be to being your brothers.

Keep those friendships cultivated. Support your friends the same way as you need their support.

We have family in church too. The members in the church are kind, encouraging and great children of God. I have no doubt that God will continue to use them to be instruments of peace, love and harmony in the house of God.

Know, too, that the friends that I have made here in Ireland are great people with good hearts and I have no doubt that they would kindly fill my shoes if need be.

Aunt Patricia and her family have been of great help. She would go out of her way to help wherever she can. Blessed's mum, Aunt Simmy, Aunt Esmerat and Banele's mum are also kind-hearted people, who will help wherever they can.

Shakillrulah's mum always celebrates your successes. She, too, is kind hearted and will go out of her way to help wherever she can.

Aunt Emma is one who asks of you all the time as well.

Mummy Zainab also asks of you and there are a lot of these kind-hearted people in the site who wish you well in life.

Always make time for your brothers as they look up to you as a role model.

Find time to pray for the above people when you say your prayers, for I know that they, too, do so for you.

Some members of Frontline Family Church

Conclusion

Eventually things worked out and we are here now.

You are in university and starting a new chapter in your life.

I want you to know that your grandparents acted the way they did because they were hurt that your dad couldn't continue to take care of them. They looked for someone to direct their anger and they did it to me.

I learnt to forgive them because they are your relatives and I had to make sure that there was always communication between you and them.

Your grandfather passed away in 2005. He was laid to rest next to your dad's grave.

Your grandmother is a humble person and I have forgiven her too for everything they put me through.

The rest of the family is the same; I encourage you to communicate with them always as they are your family.

Forgiveness is very important.

Uncle TC always asks about that is why I told you to call him on Christmas day.

Kollourous is a friend of mine on Facebook. He, too, always asks about you.

I communicate with Uncle Sydney now and then. I have forgiven him too.

Some of your dad's friends never thought that we would make it this far, but we did and you know what? We will go farther.

Keep believing in yourself, son, and never look back.

I want you to know that you can do anything you set your mind on. You will be successful and you will be a good husband and father one day.

You have a lot of role models around you, like your Business teacher, who always had time for you.

Ecclesiastes 3:4-5

A time to weep, and a time to laugh,
A time to mourn and a time to dance,
A time to scatter stones and a time to gather them,
A time to embrace and a time to refrain from embracing.

I must move on. I am sure that it is what your dad would have wanted me to do and you should support me on it.

I wish you all the best in your college years and remember to always show respect to everyone you meet.

I love you and I am so proud of how far you have come.